Great African Americans

Paul Robeson

a voice to remember

Revised Edition

Patricia and Fredrick McKissack

Series Consultant
Dr. Russell L. Adams, Chairman
Department of Afro-American Studies, Howard University

Enslow Publishers, Inc.

40 Industrial Road   PO Box 38
Box 398   Aldershot
Berkeley Heights, NJ 07922   Hants GU12 6BP
USA   UK

http://www.enslow.com

To the Noltes: Larry, Sharon, Graham, and Hannah

Revised edition of Paul Robeson: A Voice to Remember © 1992.

Library of Congress Cataloging-in-Publication Data

McKissack, Pat, 1944–
    Paul Robeson : a voice to remember / Patricia and Fredrick
McKissack.— Rev. ed.
       p. cm. — (Great African Americans series)
    Includes index.
    Summary: Examines the life of the twentieth-century African-American singer and
actor who spoke out against racism and injustice.
    ISBN-10: 0-7660-1674-9
    1. Robeson, Paul, 1898–1976—Juvenile literature. 2. Afro-Americans—Biography—Juvenile literature.
3. Actors—United States—Biography—Juvenile literature. 4. Singers—United States—Biography—
Juvenile literature. 5. Political activists—United States—Biography—Juvenile literature. [1. Robeson,
Paul, 1898–1976. 2. Actors and actresses. 3. Singers. 4. Afro-Americans—Biography.] I. McKissack,
Fredrick. II. Title. III. Series: McKissack, Pat, 1944– Great African Americans series.
E185.97.R63 M35 2000
782'.0092—dc21
    [B]   00-008294

ISBN-13: 978-0-7660-1674-3

Printed in the United States of America

10 9 8 7 6

To Our Readers: We have done our best to make sure all Internet addresses in this book were active and appropriate when we went to press. However, the author and the publisher have no control over and assume no liability for the material available on those Internet sites or on other Web sites they may link to. Any comments or suggestions can be sent by e-mail to comments@enslow.com or to the address on the back cover.

Every effort has been made to locate all copyright holders of material used in this book.
If any errors or omissions have occurred, corrections will be made in future editions of this book.

Photo Credits: Courtesy of the Library of Congress, p. 26; Courtesy of the Westfield Historical Society, Westfield, New Jersey, pp. 6, 7; Harris & Ewing/Washington Star Collection, Courtesy Washingtoniana Division, D. C. Public Library, p. 24; New York Public Library, Astor, Lenox and Tilden Foundations, p. 18; Prints and Photographs Department, Moorland-Spingarn Research Center, Howard University, p. 27; Special Collections and University Archives, Rutgers University Libraries, pp. 4, 8, 10, 11, 15, 21, 23; Wisconsin Center for Film and Theater Research, pp. 3, 14, 16, 19, 20.

Cover Photos: Special Collections and University Archives, Rutgers University Libraries; Westfield Historical Society; Wisconsin Center for Film and Theater Research.

TABLE OF CONTENTS

PauL RobesoN
April 9, 1898–January 23, 1976

CHAPTER 1

Growing Up in New Jersey

aul Leroy Robeson was born on April 9, 1898. His father, William, was fifty-three years old. His mother, Maria, couldn't see well. And it was hard for her to breathe at times.

The Robesons already had four children: Bill Jr., Reeve, Ben, and Marion. Paul's older brothers and sister helped take care of him.

Paul's father, William Robeson, was born a slave. William ran away to freedom when he was fifteen years old. He worked hard and studied for

5

many years. Then he met and married Paul's mother, Maria Louise Bustill. The Robesons moved to Princeton, New Jersey. William, who was now the Reverend William Robeson, was asked to be the pastor at a church there.

While they were living in Princeton, a terrible thing happened to the Robeson family. In January 1904, Paul's mother was cleaning house. A hot coal fell from the stove, and it set Maria Robeson's skirt on fire. She died a few hours later from the burns.

St. Luke's A.M.E. Zion Church was built in 1908 by William Robeson and his congregation.

Paul was just six years old, so he never remembered much about his mother. He and his father became very close. Paul's father taught him to never quit. "My father was the most important person in my life," Paul said many years later.

6

Paul Robeson, front, with the Westfield baseball team.

Reverend Robeson was the pastor of the same church in Princeton for twenty years. After Maria's death, Reverend Robeson moved on to other churches, first in Westfield and then in Somerville, New Jersey.

**Paul played football in high school and college.
At that time, the players wore flimsy helmets and uniforms
with little padding.**

CHAPTER 2

Robesons Don't Quit!

P aul did well in sports and music at Somerville High School. He also had the lead part in the play *Othello*. *Othello* is a famous play written by William Shakespeare.

Acting scared Paul. After he played the part of Othello, he never wanted to act again.

Paul studied hard. His grades were the highest in his class. His grades were so high that Rutgers College in New Jersey wanted him to go to school there.

Paul wondered if he would be happy at Rutgers.

Paul (third from left) was a star football player, and he was also a scholar. He graduated at the top of his class, and he was a member of the Phi Beta Kappa Honor Society.

Only one other black student went there. Paul talked it over with his family. Then he decided to try it.

Paul tried out for the football team at Rutgers. Some of the white players didn't want a black player on the team. They pushed Paul very hard. They fell on him, kicked his ribs, and stepped on his fingers. They even broke his nose!

Paul hurt all over. He stayed in bed for a few days. He wanted to quit. Ten days passed. Then he remembered how his father and brothers always stood up for what was right. Would they quit? No!

Paul went back out on the football field. This time he fought back when the other players tried to hurt him. Paul was angry and very strong! He picked up one of the players and held him up in the air. He was going to slam him to the ground. The coach yelled at him to stop. Paul did. The coach said Paul was on the team.

Paul was a good football player, and he played other sports well, too. Still, he never forgot to study. He finished Rutgers with the highest grades in the class of 1919.

Paul gave a speech at his Rutgers graduation ceremony in 1919.

Paul felt happy and sad at graduation. His brothers and sister were there to hear him give the class speech. His father was not. Reverend Robeson had died the year before. But Paul knew he would have been proud.

**Paul was a very happy person. His eyes sparkled
when he shared a funny story with friends. He loved to talk,
and people enjoyed listening to him.**

CHAPTER 3

Acting for Fun

After he left Rutgers, Paul studied law at Columbia University in New York City. On weekends and in the summers he played professional football.

Paul met Eslanda Goode when she was also a student at Columbia. Everybody called her Essie. She wanted to be a doctor.

It didn't take long for Essie and Paul to fall in love. In August 1921, they slipped off to Rye, New York, and were married. Paul finished law school in 1923.

In the 1920s, it was very hard for a black man to be accepted as a lawyer. But Paul felt lucky. A white lawyer asked him to join his law firm.

Paul expected to be treated fairly, but he was not. The white lawyers did not want to work with him. A white secretary would not work for him. At last his boss asked Paul to open a law office in Harlem. Harlem is a mostly black neighborhood in New York City.

Paul was the third African American to graduate from Columbia Law School.

Paul told Essie what happened. She was very angry. She told him not to take the job. He was six feet tall. He was strong and very good looking. He looked like an actor. Why not be one?

Essie talked Paul into taking part in a YMCA play. He tried it just for fun. But he had not forgotten how frightening acting had been in high school.

Paul found that he liked acting. One of his most famous roles was in *Emperor Jones*. He starred in the 1924 stage play by Eugene O'Neill, and later in the film version.

Paul did very well in the play. He began to take other parts in plays. "I was being paid . . . to walk on stage, say a few lines, sing a song or two," Paul said later. "Just too good for words."

Paul was becoming popular as an actor and a singer.

C H A P T E R 4

A Big, Booming Voice

t first, not many people knew how well Paul could sing. He enjoyed hearing and singing the spirituals he had heard in his father's church. Often he sang for friends.

One day, Paul saw an old friend named Lawrence Brown. Lawrence played the piano. Paul and Lawrence told Essie about an idea they had. They wanted to give a concert. Essie thought it was a good idea, so she helped.

Paul wondered if people would come to hear

17

**Paul
often
performed
with piano
player
Lawrence
Brown.**

him sing spirituals. He got his answer on Sunday, April 19, 1925. Paul sang to a full house at the Greenwich Village Theater in New York. Every seat was taken.

In *Emperor Jones*, Paul played a railroad porter who becomes king of a Caribbean island.

Paul was becoming a star. His fans talked about his big, booming voice. Paul's voice made people laugh and cry. When he finished singing, they stood up and cheered.

While Paul was on a singing tour in London, his son, Paul Jr., was born. Essie said she knew Paul was a healthy baby because he had a big, booming voice—just like his father.

Paul still took parts in plays. When *Show Boat* opened in London in April 1928, Paul was the star. He sang a powerful and beautiful

19

**Paul acted in many plays and films in the
United States and London, England.**

song called "Ol' Man River." This became his special song.

Then Paul was asked to play the part of Othello. The star who would play his wife was a white actress. Many people did not like that she was white and he was black. But on May 29, 1930, the play opened at the Savoy Theater in London, England.

Many people in the United States did not like the idea of Paul acting with a white actress, either. Paul was not asked to play the part of Othello with a white actress in the United States until 1943.

Paul starred as Othello in the play by William Shakespeare.

CHAPTER 5

The People's Hero

frican Americans still didn't have equal rights in the 1930s. They were treated unfairly in the theater, too. There were not many parts for black actors. Many of the roles made African Americans look foolish. Paul wouldn't take those parts. That's why the Robesons lived in London, England, and Paris, France, most of the time. He was treated fairly in those cities.

In 1939, the Robesons came back to the United States to live. World War II was about to start.

Paul was a big success. Everywhere he went, fans gathered around him. He was always willing to give autographs.

Paul spoke out about how the Jews were being treated unfairly in Germany. He said that African Americans were not treated any better in the United States. He also said America needed to change, so that all people would be treated fairly.

23

After the war, any American who was friendly with the Soviet Union or Communists got into trouble. Paul was one of them. He had been to the Soviet Union on concert tours. The people enjoyed his music very much. He said, "I am treated like a human being in the Soviet Union. I am not in the United States."

In the 1950s, a group of senators accused many Americans of being Communists. Essie (above) and Paul were questioned. In protest, they refused to answer.

The United States government did not like what Paul was saying. A lot of Americans thought he was a traitor. After one of his concerts, there was a terrible riot. People threw rocks and bottles at those who had come to hear him sing.

By 1950, the United States government would not let Paul or Essie travel outside the country. Nobody would hire him to make a

Paul and several other performers gave a concert in Peekskill, New York, in 1949. Some people believed Paul was a traitor because he spoke out for civil rights. There was a riot and many people were attacked as they left the concert. Paul barely got away.

movie or be in a play. Still Paul didn't give up. He fought for his rights and the rights of others, too.

"All I want is a good America for all its people," Paul said. Paul Robeson didn't quit. He spoke up for what he believed to be right. Some

Paul won many awards for his music and for his work on behalf of human rights all over the world. Here he is receiving the Star of Friendship of the People from East German president Walter Ulbricht in 1960.

people feared Paul. Others loved him. He was a hero to many people all over the world.

At last, in 1958, he and Essie won an important

court case. A judge said they could travel outside the country. They left the United States. They lived in the Soviet Union, London, and Paris. Paul gave concerts all over the world, but he didn't give any in America.

In 1963, the Robesons came back to the United States. America was changing. Paul was very lonely when Essie died two years later. He stopped singing and acting, but he never stopped speaking out for equal rights.

Paul Robeson died in January 1976. Thousands of people came to his funeral in Harlem. Paul Robeson is remembered by many people as a great singer and actor. Others honor him for his courage. He fought for equal rights when other people were too afraid to try.

This sculpture was created by Russian sculptor Bernice Marker to honor the memory of Paul Robeson.

timeLine

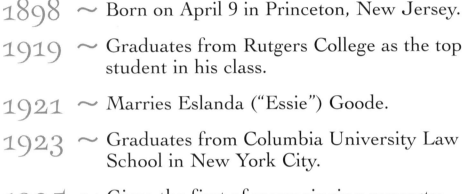

1898 ~ Born on April 9 in Princeton, New Jersey.

1919 ~ Graduates from Rutgers College as the top student in his class.

1921 ~ Marries Eslanda ("Essie") Goode.

1923 ~ Graduates from Columbia University Law School in New York City.

1925 ~ Gives the first of many singing concerts; stars in *The Emperor Jones* in London.

1928 ~ Opens in *Show Boat* in London.

1930 ~ Stars in *Othello* in London.

1943 ~ Stars in *Othello* on Broadway.

1940s ~ Speaks out for civil rights and angers the U.S. government.

1950 ~ Is not allowed to travel outside the U.S.

1958 ~ Is allowed to travel, and lives abroad. Goes on an international concert tour.

1963 ~ Returns to the United States.

1976 ~ Dies on January 23.

1943

953

919

WORDS TO KNOW

All-American—An athlete who is one of the top college players in the country during the year. Paul was an All-American football player at Rutgers College for two years in a row.

Communists—Those who believe in the form of government that was practiced in the Soviet Union. Factories, farms, and other businesses are all owned by the government and shared by all the people.

concert—A musical show.

discrimination—To be treated unfairly.

graduate—To complete studies at a school. Paul graduated from Rutgers College in 1919.

Harlem—A large neighborhood of African Americans in New York City. In the 1920s, many famous black actors, writers, and musicians lived in Harlem.

professional football—Organized football games where players are paid to be part of a team.

riot—Violent acts that are done by a mob of people.

secretary—A person who manages the day-to-day operations of an office, or assists others in their work.

WORDS to KNOW

slave—A person who is owned by another person and forced to work without pay.

Soviet Union—In the 1950s, the Soviet Union was a very large and powerful communist country. It was located partly in Europe and partly in Asia. In 1991, the Soviet Union was divided into many separate countries. The largest one is Russia.

spirituals—Religious songs that were first sung by black slaves.

traitor—A person who works against his or her country.

World War II—A war that was fought in Europe, North Africa, and Asia from 1939 to 1945. The United States entered World War II in 1941, and it united with Great Britain, China, the Soviet Union, and other nations to fight against Nazi Germany, Japan, and Italy.

YMCA—The initials are for the Young Men's Christian Association, a group that offers classes, sports, shows, and other activities.

Learn more about Paul Robeson

Books

Ehrlich, Scott. *Paul Robeson: Athelete, Singer, Activist.* Los Angeles, Calif.: Holloway House Publishing Company, 1989.

Greenfield, Eloise. *Paul Robeson.* New York, N.Y.: Harper Collins Children's Books, 1975

Plumpp, Sterling. *Paul Robeson.* Chicago, Ill.: Third World Press, 1992.

Recordings

Ballad for Americans (Vanguard, 1990)

The Odyssey of Paul Robeson (Vanguard Classics, 1998)

Paul Robeson Favorite Songs, Vol. 1 (Monitor Records, 1992)

Internet Addresses

Paul Robeson's Celebration
<http://picpal.com/robesonb.html>

Paul Robeson Centennial Celebration
<http://www.cpsr.cs.uchicago.edu/robeson>

index

a
African Americans,
    rights of, 22, 23,
    24–25

B
Brown, Lawrence, 17

C
Columbia University, 13
Communists, 24
concerts, 17, 19, 24
    riot at, 24

H
Harlem, 14, 27

L
London, England, 19,
    21, 22, 27

N
New York City, 13–14,
    19

O
"Ol' Man River," 21
Othello, 9, 21

P
Paris, France, 22, 27
Princeton, New Jersey,
    6–7

R
Robeson, Ben, 5, 11
Robeson, Bill Jr., 5, 11
Robeson, Eslanda
    Goode, 13–14, 17,
    19, 26–27
Robeson, Maria Louise
    Bustill, 5–7
Robeson, Marion, 5, 11
Robeson, Paul L.
        as actor, 9, 14, 16,
        19, 21, 26–27
        birth of, 5
        death of, 27
        as football player,
        10–11
        marriage, 13
        as singer, 17, 19,
        21, 27
        as student, 9, 11
        speaks for rights
        of African
        Americans, 23,
        24–25, 27

Robeson, Paul Jr., 19
Robeson, Reeve, 5, 11
Robeson, the Reverend
    William, 5–7, 11
Rutgers College, 9, 11,
    13

S
Savoy Theater, 21
Shakespeare, William, 9
Show Boat, 19
Somerville, New Jersey,
    7, 9
Soviet Union, 24, 27
spirituals, 17, 19

u
United States, 21,
    22–24, 27

w
World War II, 22
Westfield, New Jersey, 7

y
YMCA, 14